*For Owen:
May your love for
life, liberty, and puppies
be exceeded only
by your love for Jesus.*

Copyright © 2026 by Krystal Heath
Artwork - AI via ChatGPT
AI rhyming assistance provided by CoPilot
First printing 2026, USA
All rights reserved, including the right of reproduction in whole or in part in any form.
ISBN-13: 979-8-9948347-0-1

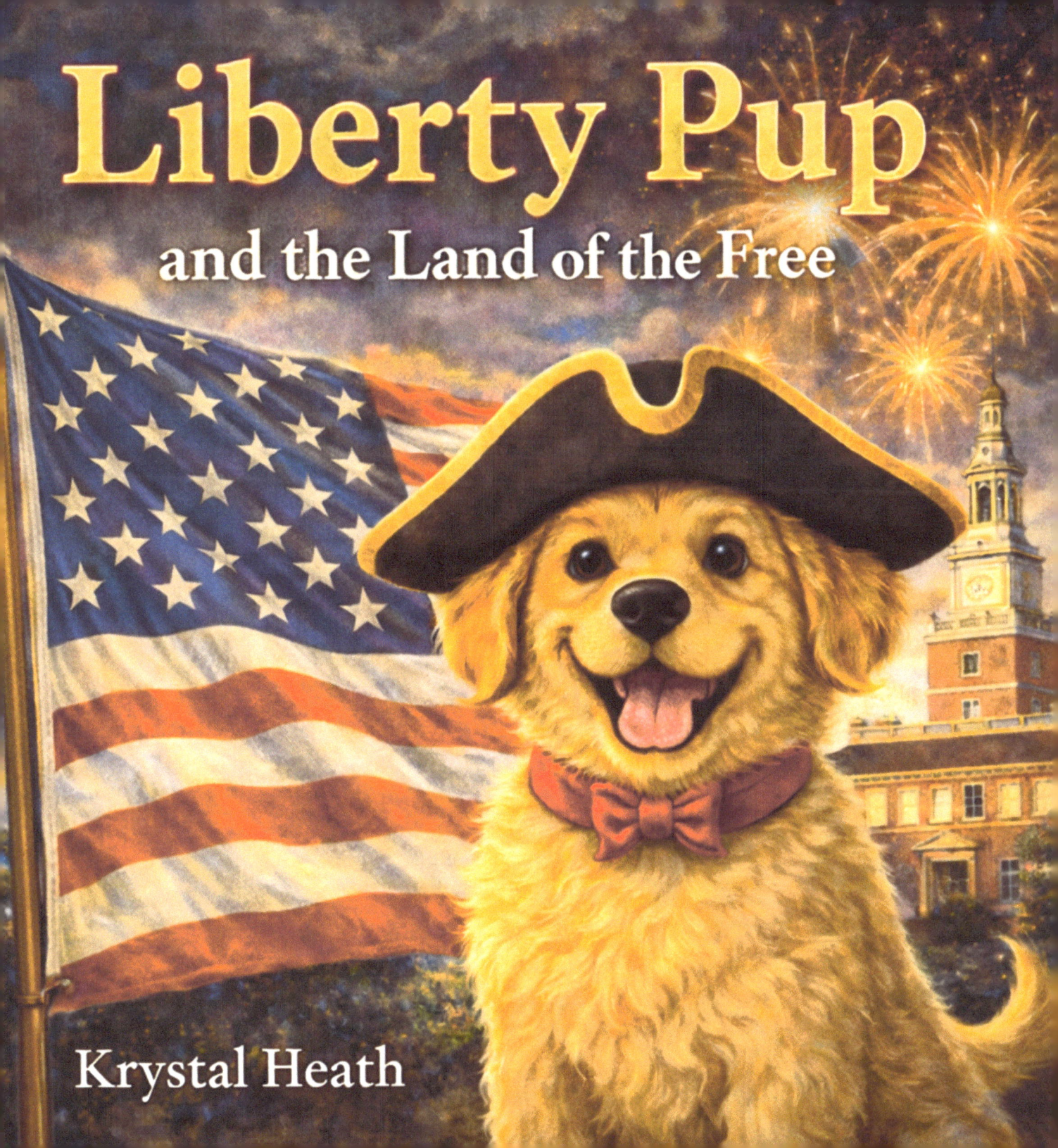

Columbus sailed in fourteen ninety-two,
not knowing what he'd find,
And reached the wide Americas,
a land not yet on maps outlined.
Many families followed after,
braving the ocean's foam,
Hoping this new world might be their future home.

The settlers in the thirteen colonies lived and grew,
Loyal to the English crown in all they had to do.

In seventeen sixty-five, the colonies felt something strange, When the King of England ordered taxes in a sweeping paper change. On newspapers, and contracts, and books the people read, Yes, even the Holy Bible had a tax upon its head! But the colonists protested, saying, "This just isn't fair! We can't be taxed by Parliament when we have no voice there!" They argued that their rights as British subjects were betrayed, And soon the Stamp Act vanished, its unjust tax no longer paid.

The King sent more soldiers
out across the sea,
Red-coated men
whose uniforms were
very bright indeed!
He ordered towns and
families to give them
food and gear,
To house them, help them,
move them - costs the
colonists held dear.
The people cried,
"This isn't right -
another tax, no less!
He's taking all our
goods and things;
it's causing real distress.
And still we have
no voice in Parliament,
where laws are cast!"
A tension that would shape
the course of history at last.

The colonists disliked
the Redcoats marching
through their towns,
For everywhere the soldiers went,
they felt the King's harsh frowns.
In Boston,
tempers flared one night -
harsh words turned into blows,
And five brave colonists were
killed when shots and chaos rose.
The tragedy was called the
"Boston Massacre" by name,
A moment that would
fill their town
with anger and disdain -
For many blamed the King
and the soldiers
he had sent,
And resolve in hearts
of colonists
grew bold in their intent.

But the King paid little mind
to what the colonists had to say,
And in 1773, he chose
a stricter way -
He ruled that only one tea
company could sell
in the new land,
And every leaf of taxed-tea trade
would follow his command.
But still the colonists had no voice
in Parliament's debate,
Where laws on what was
taxed were set
and sealed their fate.

A group of daring colonists, the "Sons of Liberty" by name,
Dressed up as native warriors when the quiet nighttime came.

They boarded ships with the King's taxed tea stacked high and deep,
And tossed it in the harbor while the town was fast asleep.
They swept the decks before they left, made sure no harm was done -
For they were there to protest the tea tax, not loot or injure anyone.
This bold and famous act, performed beneath the moonlit sea,
Would soon be known forever as the "Boston Tea Party."

The Boston Tea Party made the King furious and grim,
So he closed the busy Boston Harbor as a punishment from him.
No ships could bring in food or goods for families by the shore,
And soon he sent more soldiers out, demanding even more.
He ordered them to hunt down those who spoke against his rule,
Who dared to call out his actions as unjust, unfair, and cruel.

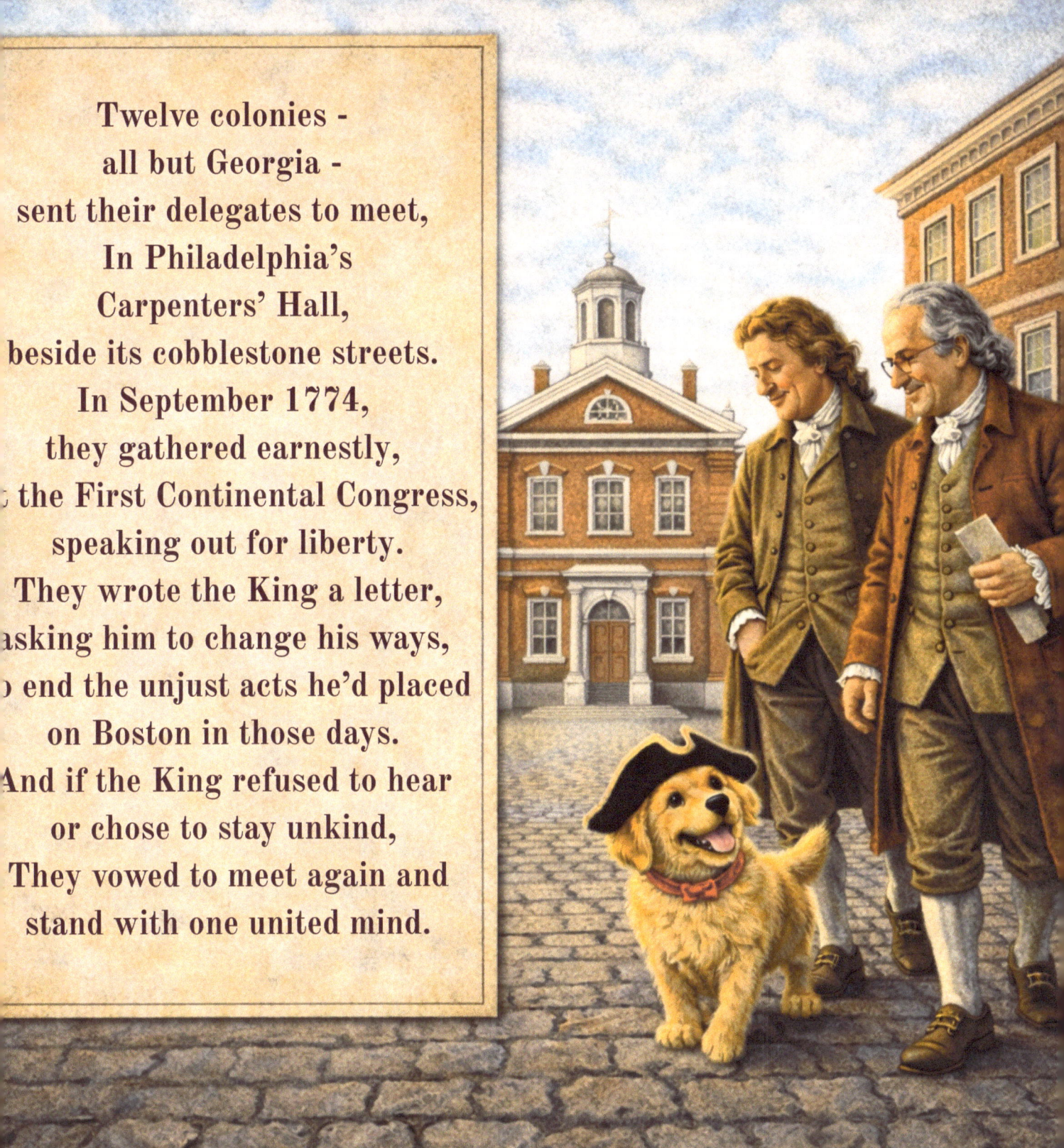

Twelve colonies -
all but Georgia -
sent their delegates to meet,
In Philadelphia's
Carpenters' Hall,
beside its cobblestone streets.
In September 1774,
they gathered earnestly,
the First Continental Congress,
speaking out for liberty.
They wrote the King a letter,
asking him to change his ways,
to end the unjust acts he'd placed
on Boston in those days.
And if the King refused to hear
or chose to stay unkind,
They vowed to meet again and
stand with one united mind.

But the King refused to listen, and in April '75,
He sent his soldiers marching out to seize two men alive -
Samuel Adams, who had stood at Congress with the rest,
And his good friend John Hancock, whom the King called "dangerous" at best.
But Paul Revere, a patriot bold, discovered Britain's plan,
And leapt upon his horse to ride as fast as one brave man can.
Through darkness toward Lexington he raced to warn his friends,
He woke them from their slumber, saving both from danger's trends.
Another rider, Samuel Prescott, sped to Concord that same night,
To warn the townsfolk there that Redcoats soon would be in sight.

When the Redcoats marched to Concord
on that April morning bright,
They found the militia waiting -
quite a startling sight!
These colonists, called minute men,
were ready on the green,
Defending rights and freedoms
they believed were just and keen.
No one knew quite what to do;
no one sought a deadly fight,
But suddenly a gun went off
and echoed through the light.
No one knows which side had fired,
or who had raised the gun,
But when that single shot rang out,
the war truly had begun.
Right there on Lexington's broad green -
and Concord's fields unfurled -
They sparked what we remember
as the shot heard 'round the world.

In May of seventeen seventy-five,
they gathered once again,
The Second Continental Congress,
a group of the colonies' best men.
In Independence Hall they spoke
of what must now be done,
And chose George Washington
as the General to lead
their militias as one.
With a united army formed
to guard their liberty,
The colonies prepared themselves
for what was soon to be.

When Washington arrived
to take command at last,
His troops moved heavy cannons
through snow and fields quite vast.
They set them on a rugged hill
overlooking Boston below,
And there they held the Redcoats fast,
with nowhere left to go.
Surrounded and outmatched at last,
the Redcoats had to flee,
And Boston was returned to
Massachusetts' colonists,
finally free.
'Twas March of seventeen seventy-six,
and news spread far and wide -
The colonists had won
their first great victory with pride!

Then Congress asked young Jefferson to write with steady hand,
A Declaration telling why they'd break from Britain's land.
On July fourth, 1776, the news rose like a cheer -
The colonies embraced his words and claimed their freedom here!
John Hancock signed his name first, in a script both large and clear,
To be sure the King could read it when the message reached his ear.

*John Hancock*

"Proclaim liberty throughout all the land unto all the inhabitants thereof." Leviticus 25:10

The Liberty Bell rang proudly from Independence Hall,
Its message echoed outward as it called to one and all.
The colonies were free at last, no longer ruled by kings;
United then as one, they claimed the hope that freedom brings.
That day the world took notice, for a brand-new nation shorn
of Britain's rule stood tall at last, The United States was born.

The King was far from happy,
and the war dragged on for years -
Five long ones after freedom's words
first reached the nation's ears.
In August seventeen seventy-six,
on Long Island's open plain,
Washington and his men
faced danger's rising strain.
Their only chance was rowing
to Manhattan's distant shore,
But British ships filled the river,
blocking them once more.
Then suddenly a fog rolled in,
a gift they hadn't planned!
And through that mist they slipped away,
a rescue heaven-sent and grand.

George Washington asked Betsy Ross to stitch a flag brand-new
A banner for the colonies in red and white and blue.
She sewed thirteen stars to honor every state,
A symbol of their unity, one hopeful, strong, and great.

It was Christmas night of seventeen seventy-six,
when Washington and his men prepared a daring fix.
They climbed into their boats to cross the icy Delaware,
A secret winter mission through the freezing midnight air.
They launched a bold surprise attack and captured Hessian foes,
German troops the English King had hired, as everybody knows.
The victory lifted spirits when the war felt dark and long,
A triumph for the colonies, determined, brave, and strong.

But still the fight it carried on,
and hope was hard to see.
By Christmas seventeen seventy-seven,
cold as cold could be,
the General and all his men
were weary, worn, and sore.
They built log cabins at Valley Forge
to wait the winter's war.
And Washington, in quiet prayer,
sought guidance from above -
For God to help his struggling troops
and bless the land they loved.

In October seventeen eighty-one,
the war at last was done.
For Cornwallis, trapped at Yorktown,
knew the patriots had won.
He surrendered to brave Washington,
no path left to escape,
A victory that changed the world
and history's very shape.
Then in the Treaty signed at Paris
in seventeen eighty-three,
The peace was made official,
America was free!

But trouble with the British crown was not yet in the past,
For in the year of 1812, new conflict rose up fast.
The British seized American men and forced them out to sea,
To serve aboard the King's warships instead of living free.

The Redcoats marched on Washington and set the town aflame.
They even burned the President's house, yet it stood, all the same.
Its walls were charred and blackened, so when peace returned once more,
They painted it a shining white to hide the scars of war.
And from that time to this, through each new term and test,
The White House has been home to every President.

In 1814, Francis Scott Key
sailed out beneath the sky,
To bargain for Americans
the British held captive nearby.
But once aboard their warship,
he was told he had to stay,
For they would strike
Fort McHenry before he'd sail away.
All night the cannons thundered
as the British fired on,
Under the rocket's red glare,
he watched and waited long.
And when the morning sunlight
broke across the harbor's span,
The Star-Spangled Banner yet waved,
o'er the brave men and their land.

Finally in December of eighteen-fourteen's cold,
The Treaty signed at Ghent brought peace, just as the year grew old.
The second war with Britain, filled with hardship, fear, and flame,
Was finally at its ending when that peace agreement came.
And with the war now over, the nation breathed anew,
Ready for the future and the dreams it would pursue.

And that's how the United States came to be, Home of liberty, the land of the free!

www.ingramcontent.com/pod-product-compliance
Lightning Source LLC
LaVergne TN
LVHW070435070526
838199LV00015B/520